Woodland Animals

Porcupines

by William John Ripple

Consulting Editor: Gail Saunders-Smith, PhD
Consultant: Daniel K. Rosenberg, Assistant Professor
College of Natural Resources, Utah State University

Capstone
press

Mankato, Minnesota

Pebble Books are published by Capstone Press,
151 Good Counsel Drive, P.O. Box 669, Mankato, Minnesota 56002.
www.capstonepress.com

1 2 3 4 5 6 11 10 09 08 07 06

Library of Congress Cataloging-in-Publication Data
Ripple, William John.
    Porcupines / by William John Ripple.
    p. cm.—(Pebble books. Woodland animals)
    Summary: "Simple text and photographs present porcupines, how they look,
where they live, and what they do"—Provided by publisher.
    Includes bibliographical references and index.
    ISBN-13: 978-0-7368-4249-5 (hardcover)
    ISBN-10: 0-7368-4249-7 (hardcover)
    1. Porcupines—Juvenile literature. I. Title. II. Series: Woodland animals.
QL737.R652R56 2006
599.35'97—dc22   2004027188

The author dedicates this book to his nephew Kail Vaith and niece Lindzie Vaith of
Lesterville, South Dakota.

Note to Parents and Teachers

The Woodland Animals set supports national science standards
related to life science. This book describes and illustrates porcupines.
The photographs support early readers in understanding the text.
The repetition of words and phrases helps early readers learn new
words. This book also introduces early readers to subject-specific
vocabulary words, which are defined in the Glossary. Early readers
may need assistance to read some words and to use the Table of
Contents, Glossary, Read More, Internet Sites, and Index sections
of the book.

Table of Contents

What Are Porcupines?

Porcupines are
large rodents with quills.
Quills are sharp,
pointy hairs.

Porcupines are dark
brown or black.
Parts of their quills
are white.

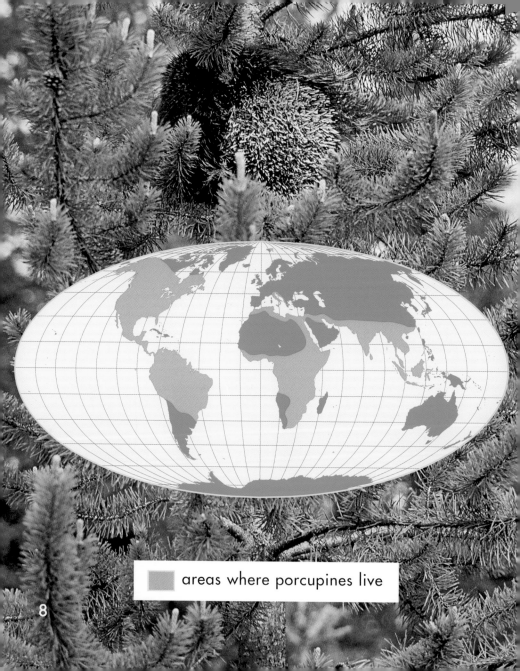

areas where porcupines live

Where Porcupines Live

Porcupines live in forests, deserts, and grasslands around the world.

Body Parts

Porcupines have
strong, sharp teeth.
They gnaw
on tree branches.

Porcupines have
long, curved claws.
Claws help porcupines
climb trees.

Each porcupine has about 30,000 quills on its back. Quills keep porcupines safe from other animals.

What Porcupines Do

Porcupines hit predators
with their quills.
Sharp quills
hurt predators.

18

Porcupines eat leaves,
bark, and branches.
They eat at night.

Porcupines rest in trees during the day.

Glossary

bark—the outside covering of a tree; bark is found both on the trunk and the branches.

desert—a very dry area of land

forest—land that is covered mostly by trees

gnaw—to chew continually on something; many rodents gnaw to wear down their teeth.

grassland—open land covered mostly by grass

predator—an animal that hunts other animals for food

quills—sharp, pointed hairs that cover a porcupine's body; each quill has tiny hooks that can stick into the skin of predators.

rodent—a small mammal with long front teeth that never stop growing; porcupines, beavers, squirrels, rats, and mice are rodents.

Read More

Knudsen, Shannon. *Prickly Porcupines.* Pull Ahead Books. Minneapolis: Lerner, 2003.

Schaefer, Lola M. *Porcupines.* Tiny-Spiny Animals. Chicago: Heinemann, 2004.

Swanson, Diane. *Porcupines.* Welcome to the World of Animals. Milwaukee: Gareth Stevens, 2002.

Internet Sites

FactHound offers a safe, fun way to find Internet sites related to this book. All of the sites on FactHound have been researched by our staff.

Here's how:

1. Visit *www.facthound.com*

2. Type in this special code **0736842497** for age-appropriate sites. Or enter a search word related to this book for a more general search.

3. Click on the **Fetch It** button.

FactHound will fetch the best sites for you!

Index

Word Count: 96
Grade: 1
Early-Intervention Level: 10

Editorial Credits
Martha E. H. Rustad, editor; Patrick D. Dentinger, set designer; Ted Williams, book
 designer; Wanda Winch, photo researcher; Scott Thoms, photo editor

Photo Credits
Bruce Coleman Inc./Gail M. Shumway, 18; George D. Dodge, 4; Joe McDonald, 20;
 John Shaw, 12; Tom Brakefield, 14
Corbis/Tom Brakefield, 10
Corel, 1
Minden Pictures/Konrad Wothe, 6; Tim Fitzharris, cover
Tom & Pat Leeson, 8, 16

24